COMMON SENSE LEADERSHIP

Practical thoughts for leaders

Sid Callaway

SHEP INSPIRES LLC

CONTENTS

Title Page

Copyright

Common Sense Leadership   1

Introduction   4

Common Sense Leaders Are Easy to Understand   5

Common Sense Leaders Prioritize Correctly   6

Common Sense Leaders   8

Common Sense Leaders   9

Common Sense Leaders   10

Common Sense Leaders   11

Common Sense Leaders   12

Common Sense Leaders   13

Common Sense Leaders   14

Common Sense Leaders   16

Common Sense Leaders   17

Common Sense Leaders   18

Common Sense Leaders   19

Common Sense Leaders   20

Common Sense Leaders   21

Common Sense Leaders   23

Common Sense Leaders   25

Common Sense Leaders   26

Common Sense Leaders   28

Common Sense Leaders   30

Common Sense Leaders are Friendly   32

Common Sense Leaders   33

Common Sense Leaders   35

Common Sense Leaders   36

Common Sense Leaders   38

Common Sense Leaders   39

Common Sense Leaders   40

Common Sense Leaders Delegate   42

Common Sense Leaders   43

Common Sense Leaders   44

Scripture References   46

The End   48

Acknowledgement   49

About The Author   51

COMMON SENSE LEADERSHIP

By: Sid Callaway

Contents

Common Sense Leaders are Easy to Understand

Common Sense Leaders Prioritize Correctly

Common Sense Leaders Are Confident

Common Sense Leaders Bless Those They Lead

Common Sense Leaders are Really Servants

Common Sense leaders are Where They're Supposed
to Be, Doing What They're Supposed to Do

Common Sense Leaders have Purpose in Everything They Do

Common Sense Leaders Use Theirs Gifts and
the Gifts of Those They Lead Wisely

Common Sense Leaders are Great Thinkers

Common Sense Leaders Care About and
Take Care of Those They Lead

Common Sense Leaders Understand that Training
Those They Lead Never Stops

Common Sense Leaders are Great Fighters

Common Sense Leaders Can Identify Other Leaders

Common Sense Leaders are Easy to Work For

Common Sense Leaders Keep It Simple

Common Sense Leaders are Constant Learners

Common Sense Leaders are Dependable

Common Sense Leaders Can Be Trusted

Common Sense Leaders Are Not Intimidated By Others Leaders

Common Sense Leaders Can Lead From Any Level

Common Sense Leaders are Friendly

Common Sense Leaders Know When to Remain Silent

Common Sense Leaders Do Not Shame or Embarrass

Common Sense Leaders Lead Themselves

Common Sense Leaders are Great Planners and Plan Ahead

Common Sense Leaders Plan, Plan and Plan

Common Sense Leaders Must Be Fit and Stay Fit

Common Sense Leaders Delegate

Common Sense Leaders Know That One of the Best
Things They Can Do Is Replace Themselves

Common Sense Leaders Know When They Are Finished
In Their Current Role and Move On

INTRODUCTION

Even though God gifts some with the gift of leadership, I believe that a lot of leadership is learned. We all have to grow and develop even if naturally gifted in an area. This book is definitely not exhaustive regarding leadership. It is not even a teaching book on leadership. It is simply some thoughts and insights on leadership that all leaders should know by way of common sense.

If you are in a leadership position then I encourage you to lead effectively, starting with the simple common sense strategies to raise those you lead to a higher level, and most of all always ask God for help.

COMMON SENSE LEADERS ARE EASY TO UNDERSTAND

Giving clear directions is a no brainer. We need to communicate in the simplest ways. To do this, we need to understand the mindset of those we lead so that we can communicate in ways they can understand using examples they can relate to.

Because I spend most of my working time with coaches and athletes it just makes sense to communicate with them in athletic terms. This way we can all be on the same page.

What good is it when a communicator doesn't realize the mindset of his/her audience? They are speaking just to hear themselves talk because the message is not transferred in the best way.
So when communicating keep it simple, keep it short, keep it relative, and keep it understandable.

COMMON SENSE LEADERS PRIORITIZE CORRECTLY

It's important that certain things get done. It is good that certain things get done. It is icing on the cake if you can get to other less important things.

Leaders usually have a lot on their plate. It seems that some are always behind, never getting to the things that matter the most. It also seems that in today's society there are more distractions than ever before. Of course, this takes our focus off more important things and moves less important things to the forefront.

You would think that all of today's technology would help us prioritize but it can be a hindrance if we don't use our electronic devises wisely.

What we have to do every day is get into the habit of handling the most important things first if possible. If this is not possible then we must block out the time to handle certain things and be very firm in not letting anything, except an emergency or something beyond our control, take or interrupt this time.

We have to plan, and execute according to importance.

Common sense leaders are naturally very good at this but everyone can learn how to do this. We have

to schedule everything out (and I mean everything),
and stick to our schedule. This includes our whole day,
our personal, family, and professional agendas.

A good idea is to prioritize everything that is important
for today and find another time for less important things.
Another benefit from this is stress reduction.

COMMON SENSE LEADERS

Are Confident

We have to be confident if we are going to lead effectively. Who wants to follow someone who is always uncertain? James 1:8 says, "A double minded person is unstable in all their ways."

However, we have to get our confidence from the right source. Phil 4:13 is often quoted when we speak of confidence. "I can do all things through Christ who strengthens me." This verse refers to the fact that we can do the will of God, not ours, because it is God doing His will through us.

Our part is to live in the plan, purpose, and mission that God has given us. It was God's will that Paul was on the ship as it crashed in the storm. When God told Paul that no one on it would be killed, he could tell the Captain not to worry, because he had heard from God.

It just makes sense to stay connected to God and make all our leadership decisions based on His will and how He is leading us. When we totally trust the, all powerful God, who made the whole universe, we have to be confident because it is in Him that we are confident. This is what we must pass along – Confidence that God is leading us as we lead.

COMMON SENSE LEADERS

Bless Those They Lead

God loves to bless His children- Psalm 84:11 says, "That God will not withhold any good thing from those who walk uprightly." God gives fish and bread, not stones and snakes. God loves to bless us. Period.

As parents love to do special things for their children, good leaders love to do things for those they lead. I've seen or experienced leaders giving time off for special situations that come unexpectedly. I've seen leaders motivate through various incentives such as, bonuses, vacations, and special dinners.

The more we do for those we lead, the more motivated those we lead will be. Even though, hopefully we do this to bless them, usually the blessings come back to us many folds.

COMMON SENSE LEADERS

Are Really Servants

Jesus washed the disciples' feet, presidents serve their nations, husbands serve their families, dads serve their children, and leaders in the workplace are really servants of those they lead.

Leaders put in time when others are sleeping, playing, relaxing, and off duty. In other words leaders usually work longer and harder than those they lead.

Leaders have to get themselves prepared before they can prepare others. You can't lead others if you aren't ahead of them. Usually we leaders have people that we lead who are sharp and disciplined. We cannot lead them from the rear. We must be in front, paving the way, setting the example, and keeping ourselves sharp so we can be the most effective that we can be.

Jesus Christ said that a servant is not greater than his master. In other words, the boss is in charge and should be worthy in every way of being in charge

When we serve we become most like Christ and the example of the greatest leader ever.

COMMON SENSE
LEADERS

<u>Are Where They're Supposed To Be,</u>
<u>Doing What They're Supposed To Do</u>

Proper positioning is very critical. Ask any sports coach, military sergeant, or law enforcement officer. We can't do our job if we are out of position.

There are great blessings out there for us. In the Bible, David found out very well the blessings and consequences of positioning. As a young man he was right where he was supposed to be when he was called upon to fight and defeat Goliath. He was obeying his Dad by going to visit his brothers who were fighting the Philistines.

David, later in life, didn't go to war when he, as king, was supposed to, and as a result, he committed at least two major sins for which he would suffer consequences the rest of his life.

When we are where we are supposed to be, doing what we are supposed to do, we will see, hear, and experience the blessing we are supposed to receive.

Even though we can sometimes recover from a mistake, we will usually suffer some type of consequence.

Obedience is key. Focus is critical. Success is important. Common sense leaders reap the benefits.

COMMON SENSE LEADERS

<u>Have Purpose in Everything They Do</u>

The words of Forrest Gump, "For no particular reason," are not words used by common sense leaders?

Common sense leaders live life on purpose and have a purpose for everything they do. They don't just float along in life taking things as they come.

They have a reason for getting up when they do, a reason for eating on the schedule they set, for the order in which they get ready, for how they plan their day, for what their priorities are, and for everything else.

For example, I get up at around 4:20am. This gives me time to read my Bible and pray, go to the gym, come home and eat a good breakfast so I don't have to rush or deal with my job and other people (they're usually asleep). Because of this, I can then start my workday alert, refreshed, focused, and on time.

Having purpose for everything leaves assuming and guessing out of the equation. Also, those that are around us will feel more confident that we can get the job done, be dependable, and that we will be where we are supposed to be.

This principle will help us in all areas of our life- health, family, work, play, recharging, and rest.

COMMON SENSE LEADERS

<u>Use Their Gifts and The Gifts of Those They Lead Wisely</u>

Play to your strengths. God gifted us with certain abilities, passions, and talents. This is one way to stay fresh and recharged.

When we spend too much time out of our gift zone we become frustrated and discouraged. Our work will drain us.

We all have to do things we don't like and take on tasks that we're not good at but if we're spending most of our time in our gift zone, we will be encouraged, energetic and fulfilled.

Someone once said, "Do what you're passionate about and you'll never work a day in your life." When we lead others we need to discern their gifts, passions, and talents also. This way we can get much more accomplished and keep those under out leadership happy and fulfilled.

So we should do the common sense thing and spend the most of our time in our strengths and keep on getting better and stronger. It will really pay off in more ways than one.

COMMON SENSE LEADERS

Are Great Thinkers

We're too busy to think. We are also too insecure to think. We are afraid of what others will think of us if we're not moving and shaking at a break neck pace. We think of work as a doing not being.

A lot of productivity has resulted from thinking. I once read in one of John Maxwell's books that an employee of a big company complained to the boss that he often saw another employee sitting and looking out a window. The boss quickly told him that on one of those experiences, that employee came up with an idea that made millions for the company.

When we move too fast we can't see all the parameters and all the details.

Thinking is a lost art. I have heard of very successful people who take an hour, half a day, a day, or a retreat just to think. I'm talking about no interruptions, no television, no media, no electronics, just their thoughts.

God made us very capable, very complex, very smart, and very creative. Our brain is capable of so much more than we can comprehend. I definitely need to get much better at thinking. So I encourage all of us to take a walk, sit in the sun, take a drive in the country, and think.

God also encourages it. He says, "Be still and know that I am God…" (Psalm 46:10).

COMMON SENSE LEADERS

Care About and Take Care of Those They Lead

If you are going to be an effective leader, people are going to be very high on your priority scale. A leader may or may not be an extravert who is the life of the party getting along with everybody, but they do really care about people, especially about those close to them.

We all show love in different ways and that's ok as long as those we lead know we care by our actions and also by our words. My dad was not an emotional, outgoing, touchy-feely person. He was not a big time communicator either. However, I never once doubted his love for me. He never let me down and always took care of me.

I hired a young man once who moved here with $14.00 in his pocket and a few clothes, that's it, no car, no savings account, no support system. It was imperative that I take good care of him way beyond training him for the job he was to do. He turned out to be not only one of the best staff under my leadership, but one of the best staff our organization has ever had. I hated to see him go, but it was time.

God had and still has great plans for him. And even though we live a great distance apart, we stay close. Caring and loving others doesn't stop.

COMMON SENSE LEADERS

Understand That Training Those They Lead Never Stops

There is Formal Training and then there is Informal Training.

Formal Training, no matter what the capacity, is the X's and O's, the fundamentals, the logistics, the standard operating procedures, the orientation, or whatever you want to call it. It involves formalities of what is expected. It is all about the hows, why's, the do's and the don'ts. It involves structure, principles, and expectations.

On the other hand, informal training is more about coming alongside those we lead, teaching and training while doing. The atmosphere is more relaxed and the student gets to watch the leader in action.

While the formal training is necessary and usually the first part of the training, the informal goes on throughout the time the employee is on the job or throughout the son's life (in a father and son relationship) and so on.

Because the leader should always be learning, the followers get to see the benefits of his or her growth. The informal aspect of training involves relationships. We tend to shine when we are poured into and encouraged. This should never stop, and as a result the follower becomes more passionate about their role and production goes way up.

COMMON SENSE
LEADERS
Are Great Fighters

In Nehemiah 4:14 – God told Nehemiah to fight
for those he cared about and to not be afraid.

Leaders have to fight sometimes. What good Dad
wouldn't fight for his children, whether a true physical fight
or standing up to someone not treating them fairly.

We need to care about our friends, family, employees,
and peers enough to go to bat for them.
We must have their backs and be a true battle
buddy if we are going to lead effectively.

I once heard of a police chief that wanted a pay raise for his
officers. After being refused, he got all the Commissioners to
meet with him and then turned the meeting over to his officers.
He did what it took to get them the compensation they deserved.

Sometimes leaders must take the heat for what
those they lead do if their mistake is not their fault or
if circumstances call for them to change the plan. We
must show others we care enough to get involved and
when we do, they will follow us no matter what.

COMMON SENSE LEADERS

Can Identify Other Leaders

It should be easy to recognize a good leader. It is especially easy if we have skills and knowledge in leadership ourselves.

This can be a good thing and this can be a bad thing. It's good to be able to recognize that those who lead us are good at what they do. It's much easier to follow a leader when we can tell that they care about those they lead.

If we have a lot of leadership skills we can pick out these qualities in others. We then become more trusting in our leadership and get along much better.

It can be a bad thing if we are a much better leader than those who lead us because we can easily become judgmental, defiant, and not follow as we should.

We are to line up under authority willingly, but we can also appeal to our leadership if they are not leading as they should.

Therefore, leading our leaders can be ok if done with the right motives and attitudes. We should strive to make them look as good as possible. We should all be growing and getting better and at the same time helping others in their growth.

COMMON SENSE
LEADERS

Are Easy to Work For

We've all seen someone that we've worked alongside get promoted to a leadership position and all of a sudden they change into someone who feels they now are supposed to boss people around, micro-manage, become strict and demanding, and distance themselves from those he or she now leads.

Common Sense should tell us that as leaders we are not any more special than anyone else. We shouldn't take ourselves too seriously. Yes, our role may have changed but we have to be respected in order to be effective.

Therefore, be easy to get along with, be quick to help others, be nice, be understanding, and be approachable. Jesus Christ led His disciples but He led while walking along side of them. If we are there for those we lead, setting a great example, it will pay off.

COMMON SENSE LEADERS

Keep It Simple

Why in the world do we tend to make things so complicated? I think we do it to make people think we are smarter, harder working, and more committed.

However, common sense tells us just the opposite. I've seen reports that were so complicated that employees spent so much time on them that they couldn't do the simplest aspect of their jobs properly.

I've also seen staff meetings go on forever about nothing. So many staff meetings are 80% ineffective. In other words, a two hour staff meeting could really be accomplished in 30 minutes or less. Longer is not better, it only bores those in the meeting and keeps employees from other important tasks. Yes, it's good to get together to have meetings, to strategize, and to fellowship, but make it effective, fast paced, and interesting. When you are finished, you are finished. Don't drag it out just to make it go for a certain time limit.

Another thing pertaining to meetings – Do not go over the designated time limit. Attention spans are depleted, people are hungry, joints are stiff from sitting, and we are no longer effective.

If leaders could understand that simple is brilliant, we'd be better off. Don't try to impress, you will only look bad.

It is always important to be yourself. If you fake it or try to act like those you admire, you'll only make yourself ineffective because you can't fool most people.

Realize God made you very special. Don't try to change what He wants to do through you.

COMMON SENSE LEADERS

Are Constant Learners

We never get there. We never know it
all. We never have it all together.

The Bible even says, "That we haven't arrived..." (Phil
3:12-15) It would be nice to get to the place where we know
all there is to know about something. (Kind of like Bubba, in
the movie Forrest Gump, who stated, "I know all there is to
know about the shrimping business."). If that were the case
we could learn all there is to learn about something and then
move on to the next thing. Before too many years we'd be
masters in all kinds of areas and when we knew all there is to
know about what we wanted to know about we could just
stop, take a break, and coast through the rest of our lives.
However, common sense tells us that we don't know
it all, never will, but must keep learning, growing,
expanding, and searching in all areas that interest us.

The world is constantly changing, methods become
obsolete, technology is expanding, people are continually being
educated, and we must keep growing or we will be left behind.

I also understand that God has gifted us all differently
and that we will not be experts in all fields, but we must
always be on a growth journey if we are to lead effectively.

You can't take others past where you are. You

can't grow without stretching yourself. We must
keep moving. There is no standing still.

COMMON SENSE LEADERS

<u>Are Dependable</u>

A great compliment that one can receive is that if he/she tells you they are going to do something you can count on it.

We do not need to go behind the leader making sure they do what they are supposed to do. We do not need to cover up their faults in this area.

Leaders must be responsible and dependable. We have to be able to trust them and have confidence in not only their ability, but in what they say, and that they will be where they are supposed to be, and do what they are supposed to do.

- Leaders should be on time always
- Leaders should return calls, email, etc. in a timely manner
- Leaders should do their jobs, answer to their supervisors, and be an example for those they lead
- Leaders should be there for those they lead
- Leaders should fill in the gaps when necessary
- Leaders should have a great track record of integrity and character

If someone cannot be depended on then it's simple – They should not be given a leadership position – Period.

COMMON SENSE
LEADERS

<u>Can Be Trusted</u>

This one is so simple. If you can't trust the one in charge, you will not follow his/her lead.

If you are one who wants to do a good job and you do your job, "as unto the Lord" (Col 3:17), you will do the right thing no matter who is in charge.

Also, if obedience to the Word of God is important, you will obey those in authority over you (1 Peter 2:13-14).

However, you will always be cautious when dealing with that particular leader. You will be careful what you say and how much you open up. You will also checkout what they say and you will not depend on them to do what they say.

I once had a boss who was always late for appointments with me. I didn't "bust it" to make it early for my appointments with him even though being on time is very important to me.

I once caught someone lying to me a couple of times, about simple things that didn't really matter, in an attempt to make himself look good rather than admitting he made a mistake. I did not have a lot of respect for that person even though I had great love for them.

Character and Integrity are very important and valuable. It will take you a lot further than talent, ability, and knowledge.

When it comes down to trust, don't take shortcuts
and be quick to admit your wrongs and faults.
Your leadership will go to all new levels.

COMMON SENSE LEADERS

Are Not Intimidated By Other Leaders

It is so easy and so natural for us to compare ourselves to others and want to be just like them.

It is also easy to be jealous of other leaders or of others in the same position as we are. For example, if you are a sprinter you can easily find yourself trying to be like another sprinter with different gifts than yours rather than going all out being who you are using your unique giftedness to glorify God.

I've seen church pastors refuse to bring in a guest speaker because they fear that the guest will be better. They may be different with different gifts, but usually not better. The key here is effectiveness. We need to be more concerned with this because effectiveness gets the job done.

Imagine attempting to be like Paul Anderson (The World's Strongest Man, who still holds the record for picking up the most weight 20 yrs after his death) when you weight 150 lbs, and can run a marathons but can't even do 20 pushups. Yes, you need to keep doing push-ups and you will keep getting a little better, but put most of your effort on running where you will be the most effective.

The bottom-line is the fact that God made you, gifted you, loves you, and wants to use you in His divine plan.

Focus on Him, His plan, and the gifts and calling on your life and life can be fun and enjoyable and also effective.

COMMON SENSE
LEADERS

Can Lead From Any Level

Leaders are leaders – Period. If you are a leader, whether your leadership qualities come natural or you have learned leadership over the years, you are called to lead.

However, many leaders are not the boss, the CEO, the Head Coach, the quarterback, or the General.

You might find yourself in a non-leader type role because of age, inexperience, being looked over, caught up in the "it's who you know" system, or being the new person on the block.

This is no excuse for not leading. What do leaders naturally do – they lead. They lead from where they are and as stated in another chapter they start with themselves. A few qualities of a leader include – integrity, discipline, relationship building, dependability, confidence, a good example, caring, taking the necessary risks, helping others grow, and much more. We can do this from any position on the team or company.

Far too often we want to be in charge and we hold back on using our leadership gifts waiting on our promotion to get started.

I once heard a message on Judges 3:31. The points were:

- Shamgar began where he was

- He used what he had
- He did what he could

Isn't that what leadership is about? If you consider yourself a leader, then I want to encourage you to start leading. If others follow then you are truly a leader.

COMMON SENSE
LEADERS ARE
FRIENDLY

Even though people have different personalities and natures, leaders must be the first to show friendship, welcome others when they're in their presence, and be nice to others.

Whether you are shy or outgoing, an introvert or extrovert, this is something the leader has to develop and eventually be good at. This will not come naturally to everyone but can be developed and improved on by everyone.

As leaders we want those under us and around us to be as comfortable as possible so they can do their jobs as efficiently as possible.

Being friendly breeds a feeling of belonging that always produces better results.

You can be friendly and firm at the same time.

COMMON SENSE LEADERS

Know When to Remain Silent

It should be known by all leaders that it is best not to talk too much. The Bible says that even a fool is counted wise when he remains silent and holds his peace. (Proverbs 17:28). The Bible also says that a person that has knowledge spares his words. (Proverbs 17:27).

My dad was a very wise, intelligent man who didn't speak much, but when he spoke it was usually very important. Therefore, I always knew that I needed to listen to him.

Those who talk too much and dominate conversations don't usually get respect, because others know that a lot of what they have to say is just talk. It is good to be asked for our opinion instead of always giving it.

Someone once said that actions speak louder than words. We tend to remember what we see and experience much more than what we hear.

Here are some good times to keep silent:

- When others are talking
- When you haven't thought through how you feel on a given subject
- When you haven't checked out how you line up with God on a matter

- When what you would say would embarrass someone
- When you could make those in authority over
you or those under your authority look bad
- When correction is in order, and you're in a public setting
- "Silence is Golden-" Common Sense
Leaders know this to be true.

COMMON SENSE LEADERS

Do Not Shame or Embarrass

This should be a "no-brainer." Leaders with good common sense don't shame or embarrass those they lead. Bosses shouldn't embarrass employees, coaches shouldn't embarrass their players, and parents shouldn't embarrass their children. Yet, it happens all the time. Why is the question? This has the opposite effect in most cases. No one likes shame or embarrassment. Everyone knows this (at least they should).

Now I'm not talking about kidding, joking and having fun with those you lead. However, you should know them well enough to know where to draw the line. Chew them out in private, correct them correctly in public, and always encourage them. You will see great results when this principle is correctly followed.

COMMON SENSE LEADERS

Lead Themselves Well

When we think of leading it usually involves a group, team, squad, shift, congregation, employees, family, or students that we are in charge of.

However before we can lead others effectively, we must lead ourselves well. I'm a firm believer that leaders must set the example of the performance that we desire from those we lead.

When my son was growing up, one of the prayers I prayed was, "God, make me the man I dream of my son becoming." I heard a preacher say that and it stuck.

If we want those we lead to live Godly lives we must live Godly lives. If we want those we lead to be educated, we must educate ourselves.

It happens, but I can't imagine a trainer who trains athletes to be totally out of shape, over-weight and never working out. The best trainer/coach is always researching the latest techniques and experimenting on themselves.

My dad was a great example of someone who led himself well. He didn't let others throw him off course. He stayed focused on his priorities and everyone around him knew his boundaries.

We have to set boundaries for our lives and stay focused. There are a lot of good opportunities always popping up in our lives, but we must pray, discern, and ask God for wisdom on what we say yes to.

We have to weigh out new possibilities and think about how they will affect us and our families, if they will take away from our main focus, leave us too tired and burned out, or if it is God's will. If so, then we will be encouraged and energized by accepting.

COMMON SENSE LEADERS

Are Great Planners and Plan Ahead

The quote, "If you fail to plan you plan to fail" is so true.

Why wait until the last minute on anything. It only adds stress, problems, and failures. From simple things like packing for a trip to major decisions like looking for a job, planning a major life event (like a wedding), or planning out where you want to be in five years, it only make sense to start planning early.

When we plan early, and plan ahead we have time to keep from making mistakes. We also can avoid forgetting major and minor details. Also, planning ahead reduces stress in a big way. When we are rushed we get moody, forgetful, and just don't do a good job.

It should be natural to plan ahead but for way too many of us, this just doesn't happen. As a result we and those around us suffer in many ways. Life is not fun anymore and the things that we should be excited about become a nightmare.

The Bible tells us to notice the ants as they plan ahead for food and shelter for the winter. We feel better and have what we need when we are on top of things.

We can all get better at this. Start now and start early. Have fun doing life.

COMMON SENSE LEADERS

Plan, Plan and Plan

When you think about it our whole lives revolves around planning. Planning is necessary to function at every aspect of life if we are going to get anything done.

Coaches plan their teams' practices and develop a game plan for competition. Preachers plan for their messages, Soldiers plan for their mission. You get the point. I even plan out my meals and time to sleep.

Planning makes everything go smoother. It doesn't always make everything go smooth. However, if we have a plan we are better prepared to make necessary adjustments when needed.

It just makes sense to plan. Those who plan get much more done and those around them can be confident that their time will not be wasted. Planners have time to fit in all the priority items that go with each day.

Think about what happens if you go to the grocery store without a list. You walk around looking for things that you might need. You have to walk down every isle. You will usually spend a lot more time than if you had a list. You will probably spend more money buying things you already have and don't need and you will probably not get everything you need resulting in a return trip. It always pays to plan.

COMMON SENSE LEADERS

<u>Must Be Fit and Stay Fit</u>

We all have at least three gauges in our lives:
Physical, Spiritual and Emotional.

We cannot expect to lead others effectively if we are
out of balance in one or more areas of our lives. Now I
understand that none of us are perfect, and we all have
struggles in all areas of our lives, but it is balance that
we must achieve most of the time in order to be fit.

It's amazing how we can be so strong in one area and falling
apart in another. I once heard a pastor tell his experience
with getting out of balance emotionally. He said that one day
he just couldn't get it together regarding preparation for a
sermon. He noticed that his chest was tight, that he couldn't
get anything down on paper, and that he just started crying
and didn't know where that was coming from. When trying to
figure it all out he concluded that he was doing great spiritually
and that his level of physical fitness was really high. He said
that he then realized that emotionally he was burned out.

What we have to do is continually recharge. Yes, we need
the big vacations but we must also have the consistent little
recharges in all our major areas so we can be fit for service. Don't
try to do all this alone. It's best to have friends, work-out partners, accountability partners, mentors, and family to help us.

Also, it is ok to take a break and re-group. Work smart, eat right, sleep right, and exercises right and you will be in it for the long haul.

COMMON SENSE
LEADERS DELEGATE

The leader can't do it all and will soon burn out if they try.

A great leadership strategy is to assess the gifts, skills, and experiences of those they lead. Turn over as much responsibility to them as possible. This will not only free the leader up to be more effective, it will empower others. Hopefully, we know better than to micro-manage (this is just plain common sense), and also people want to be trusted with responsibility. It is great to know when you are trusted to do a good job. Everyone wants to be trusted with responsibility.

Even when you know you can do a certain task well, it is still good to give that responsibility to others. You will see great benefits as a result. I'm not saying that we don't expect and inspect. John Maxwell once said, "They won't respect what we don't inspect."

Accountability is very necessary and the leader must hold his/her staff to the standard expected. When we use this quality of delegation we are able to operate from a recharged state and much more gets done.

COMMON SENSE LEADERS

Know That One of the Best Things They Can Do Is Replace Themselves

This is common sense. We are all replaceable. The sooner we recognize this, the better.

Someone said we should all be working ourselves out of a job. When we do this it stretches us because we get to move on to other responsibilities that God has for us.

This can be within the same organization. Hopefully we want to see our workplace grow, expand, get better, reach more people, and soar to new heights. When we rise up new leaders on a continual basis we do just that.

Sometimes God calls us to a new situation where our influence and leadership can expand to a new team or workplace. After all, we should be in this thing of life to live it with others and to pour into others and to be poured into by others.

We shouldn't be intimated by sharp new people under our authority. Let them challenge you in your growth. Pour into them so they can replace you or other leaders as we all grow together.

COMMON SENSE
LEADERS

Know When They Are Finished
In Their Current Role and Move On

This is why working to replace yourself is so important.
God can move the leader on to lead somewhere else
within or without the organization or team. The
question is, "How do I know when I'm finished?" This
is a huge question with no direct answer.

However, there are some indications that
can help us through the process.

Someone we trained and mentored appears to
be ready to step up if given the opportunity.
Our passion for the role we're in has somewhat diminished.
(Fires can be rekindled but in this case we feel ready to move on.)
We have opportunities and offers elsewhere.
We are challenged by others to stretch ourselves
and take a risk.
We have become ineffective. Other possibilities
are confirmed by our family and closest friends.
We discern that God is leading us to move on.

This list is not exhaustive, but does give several insights into
ways to make a decision. We seem to know when we are finished
with something; when this particular season of our life is over.

Some people like change but for some, change is hard.

A good leader knows themself well and with God's help, can make the right decision for the right reason.

SCRIPTURE REFERENCES

As stated earlier a lot of leadership is common sense. We are also to learn leadership principles as we grow in maturity. We do this by asking good questions, studying the lives of leaders and successful people, reading good books on leadership, reflection on our own journey, and of course reading and studying God's Word.

Leadership includes many aspects we need to be effective. Some of these are: character, courage, risk taking, commitment, planning, sacrifice, confidence, humility, integrity, obedience, discipline, encouragement, focus, vision, wisdom, and dependence on God.

Listed below are a few Scripture verses that will help us grow as leaders.

The Old Testament:

Genesis 4: 6-7, 6:22, 39:6, 39:7-1 Joshua 6: 1-27, 8:1-9
Judges 4:4-23
1 Samuel 9:15-10:1, 24:1-22, 26:1-25
2 Samuel 5:17-25, 16:5-14, 22:1-51
1 Kings 4:29-34, 18:21, 18:36
2 Kings 18:36, 22:11-13, 18-19
2 Chronicles 20:1-29
Nehemiah 2:17-20
Ester 4:9-17
Job 1:1, 1:20-22, 2:3, 2:9-10
Psalms 1:16
Proverbs 1:2-5, 1:7, 11:3, 24:13-14,   27:17
Ecclesiastes 3:9-14, 9:16-18
Jeremiah 1:5-10, 29:10-14
Daniel 1:8, 3: 17-18
Habakkuk 2:2
Zechariah 11:17

The New Testament:

Matthew 3:11, 5:1-12, 6:33, 23:36-46
Luke 18:9-14
Acts 5:29, 20:32-36, 27:25
2 Corinthians 11:21-30
Philippians 1:3-6, 1:12-14, 2:13, 3:7-9,   3:13-14, 4:8
Colossians 1:9-14
1 Thessalonians 1:2, 2:11
1 Timothy 1:1-4, 1:12-17, 3:1
1 John 5:11-13

THE END

ACKNOWLEDGEMENT

I thank Jesus Christ for all the opportunities He has given me.

This book was inspired by a young man I had the priviledge to work with and mentor, C.L. "SHEP" Shepherd. Shep has been an inspiration to me in many ways. I noticed in him as a college football player, great leadership abilities. I said to myself, "One day I would be greatly blessed to bring him to the Atlanta area to work with me." God worked it out and I never regretted it. We were talking one day and I mentioned the phrase "Common Sense Leadership." Shep immediately said, "You ought to write a book by that title some day." Shep has and cntinues to add great value to my life.

ABOUT THE AUTHOR

Sid Callaway

Sid grew up in Stockbridge, GA. He was a walk-on football player at the University of Georgia.

After graduation he worked in law enforcement in Athens, GA. Later to be on staff with Fellowship of Christian Athletes and a Reserve Deputy with the Henry County Sheriff's Office.

His wonderful wife of 40 years, LuAnn is a Ph.D counselor in private practice who has inspired and helped veterans, 1st responders, pastors, teachers, business leaders, military brass and more.

Their son, Jacob is a two-time combat veteran and a current law enforcement officer. He and his wife, Alex, have a daughter, Hope-Ann. Jacob is a true American hero.

This book was written in 2016. Since then, while performing his duties as a Deputy Sheriff, Sid was shot while serving a warrant (February 9, 2018) and was critically injured. As of 2021, he is still on medical leave from the department.

www.ingramcontent.com/pod-product-compliance
Lightning Source LLC
Chambersburg PA
CBHW061159040426
42445CB00013B/1740